Langenscheidt

French
at your Fingertips

Tien Tammada

Langenscheidt

Foreword

Traveling to foreign or distant lands is a wonderful and exciting thing to do. In fact, it probably features top of the list in worldwide rankings.

However, before every journey to a foreign country, there is a hurdle to be passed and this hurdle is called "foreign languages". For many, this hurdle seems insurmountable. As a result, they have to give up their life's dream.

What a pity!

You may be planning a week's holiday in France to experience the magical countryside or considering moving to live and work in a French-speaking country. You might want to flirt or just understand when someone is trying to flirt with you (after all, you don't want to miss the chance to meet the prince or princess of your dreams, do you?).

Whatever your motivation, don't wait.
Don't let this hurdle stop you from fulfilling your lifelong dreams!
Take courage to embark on this exciting journey to learning the French language – **now!**

Once you've made the decision, you'll find that this book provides you with the first helpful steps. You don't need to book a language course and you don't need to worry yourself about complicated grammatical points.

Anyone who has learnt to master a foreign language knows that the essential and really crucial thing about learning a language is actually quite simple: you need to jump in at the deep end. Once you're in the water, everything flows from there.

Jump and don't think twice! You'll learn by doing, not by preparing. The pictures, the selection of important words and useful phrases that you'll find in this book are an important first step. As soon as you come up against the first language hurdle, you can open the book at the appropriate page and find the necessary words and phrases.

If that doesn't work, try pointing to the relevant picture or sentence with your finger. People will know immediately what you mean. It's really all very easy and convenient. That's why the book is called **"French at your Fingertips"**.

Content

Useful daily conversations

Les expressions courantes [lez‿ɛkspʀɛsjõ kurãt]

Greeting

Se saluer [sə salɥe]

Bonjour !	**Bonsoir !**	**Salut !**
[bõʒuʀ]	[bõswaʀ]	[saly]
Good morning!	Good evening!	Hello!

Comment ça va ?

[kɔmã sa va]

How are you?

Ça va bien, merci.

[sa va bjɛ̃ mɛʁsi]

I'm fine, thank you.

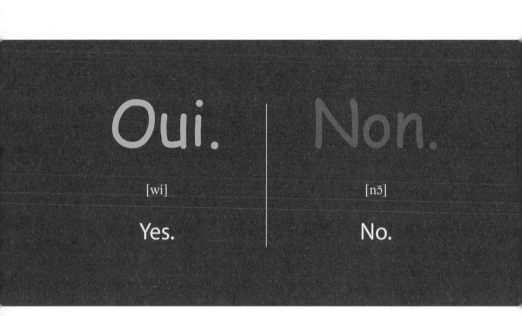

Oui.	Non.
[wi]	[nɔ̃]
Yes.	No.

Merci.	Merci beaucoup.	De rien.	Avec plaisir.
[mɛʁsi]	[mɛʁsi boku]	[də ʁjɛ̃]	[avɛk pleziʁ]
Thanks.	Thank you very much.	You're welcome.	With pleasure.

Je m'appelle … [ʒə mapɛl]	My name is …
Comment vous appelez-vous ? [kɔmɑ̃ vuz‿apəle vu]	What is your name? (formal)
Comment tu t'appelles ? [kɔmɑ̃ ty tapɛl]	What is your name? (informal)
Enchanté / Enchantée. [ɑ̃ʃɑ̃te]	Nice to meet you.
Je viens d'Etats-Unis. [ʒə vjɛ̃ dalmaɲ]	I'm from the United States.
Je ne parle pas français. [ʒə nə paʀl pa fʀɑ̃sɛ]	I don't speak French.
Je parle un peu français. [ʒə paʀl ɛ̃ pø fʀɑ̃sɛ]	I speak a little French.
Est-ce que vous pouvez parler moins vite, s'il vous plaît ? [ɛs‿kə vu puve paʀle mwɛ̃ vit sil vu plɛ]	Could you speak a little more slowly, please?
Comment ça s'appelle en français ? [kɔmɑ̃ sa sapɛl ɑ̃ fʀɑ̃sɛ]	How do you say that in French?

Qu'est-ce que ça veut dire ? [kɛs_kə sa vø diʀ]	What does that mean?
Qu'est-ce que c'est ? [kɛs_kə se]	What is that?
C'est quoi ? [se kwa]	What's that?
Pardon ! [paʀdɔ̃]	Excuse me!
Je suis désolé(e). [ʒə sɥi dezɔle]	I'm sorry.
Aucun problème. [okɛ̃ pʀɔblɛm]	No problem.
Pas de problème. [pad pʀɔblɛm]	No problem.
Monsieur ... [məsjø]	Mister ...
Madame ... [madam]	Mrs ...

Mademoiselle ... [madmwazɛl]	Miss ...
Où est ... ? [u ɛ]	Where is...?
Je voudrais ... [ʒə vudʀɛ]	I would like...
Ça coûte combien ? [sa kut kɔ̃bjɛ̃]	How much does it cost?
bien [bjɛ̃]	good
très bien [tʀɛ bjɛ̃]	very good
Ça me plaît. [sa mə plɛ]	I like this.
Ça ne me plaît pas. [sa nə mə plɛ pa]	I don't like that.
Comme ci comme ça. [kɔm si kɔm sa]	So-so.

Magnifique ! [maɲifik]	Wonderful!
Remarquable ! [ʀəmaʀkabl]	Great!
Merveilleux ! [mɛʀvɛjø]	Marvelous!
mauvais [mɔvɛ]	bad
beaucoup [boku]	a lot
un peu [ɛ̃ pø]	some, a little bit
Un moment, s'il vous plaît. [ɛ̃ mɔmɑ̃ sil vu plɛ]	One moment, please.
Un instant, s'il vous plaît. [ɛ̃nɛ̃stɑ̃ sil vu plɛ]	Just a moment, please.
A bientôt. [a bjɛ̃to]	See you soon!
A tout à l'heure. [a tut a lœʀ]	See you later!

A demain. [a dəmɛ̃]	See you tomorrow!
Au revoir. [o ʀəvwaʀ]	Good bye!
Qui ? [ki]	Who?
Quoi ? [kwa]	What?
Où ? [u]	Where?
Où est ... ? [u ɛ]	Where is...?
Où sont ... ? [u sɔ̃]	Where are...?
Quand ? [kɑ̃]	When?
Pourquoi ? [puʀkwa]	Why?
Comment ? [kɔmɑ̃]	How?
Combien ? [kɔ̃bjɛ̃]	How much? / How many?

l'aéroport
[laeʀopɔʀ]

the airport

Où est le contrôle de sécurité ?
[u ɛ lə kɔ̃tʀol de sekyʀite]

Where is the security control?

L'AVION [lavjɔ̃]

Excusez-moi, comment est-ce que je peux me rendre au centre-ville ?
[ɛkskyze mwa kɔmɑ̃ ɛs‿kə ʒə pø mə ʀɑ̃dʀ o sɑ̃tʀ vil]
Excuse me, how can I get to the city centre?

Où est la gare ?
[u ɛ la gaʀ]
Where is the train station?

[sɔʀti]
Exit

Excusez-moi,
où est la sortie ?
[ɛkskyze mwa u ɛ la sɔʀti]

Excuse me, where is the exit?

the airplane

Où est l'arrêt de bus ?
[u ɛ laʀɛ də bys]
Where is the bus stop?

Où est-ce que je peux trouver un taxi ?
[u ɛs‿kə ʒə pø tʀuve ɛ̃ taksi]
Where can I get a taxi?

Où se trouve l'office du tourisme ?
[u sə tʀuv lɔfis dy tuʀism]
Where is tourist information?

Est-ce que le centre-ville est loin ?
[ɛs‿kə lə sãtʀəvil ɛ lwɛ̃]
How far is it to the city centre?

Vous connaissez un hôtel bon marché ?
[vu kɔnɛsez ɛ̃ nɔtɛl bɔn maʀʃe]
Can you recommend an inexpensive hotel?

Pouvez-vous me conduire à cette adresse ?
[puve vu mə kɔ̃dɥiʀ a sɛt‿adʀɛs]
Would you please drive me to this address?

le taxi
[lə taksi]

taxi

Combien coûte la course ?
[kɔ̃bjɛ̃ kut la kuʀs]
How much does the ride cost?

Est-ce que je peux payer par carte de crédit ?
[ɛs‿kə ʒə pø peje paʀ kaʀt də kʀedi]
Can I pay by credit card?

Pouvez-vous me dire quand je dois descendre, s'il vous plaît ?
[puve vu mə diʀ kɑ̃ ʒdwa desɑ̃dʀ sil vu plɛ]
Could you tell me when to get off please?

Merci beaucoup pour votre aide.
[mɛʀsi boku puʀ vɔtʀ‿ɛd]
Thank you very much for your help.

le bus
[lə bys]

bus

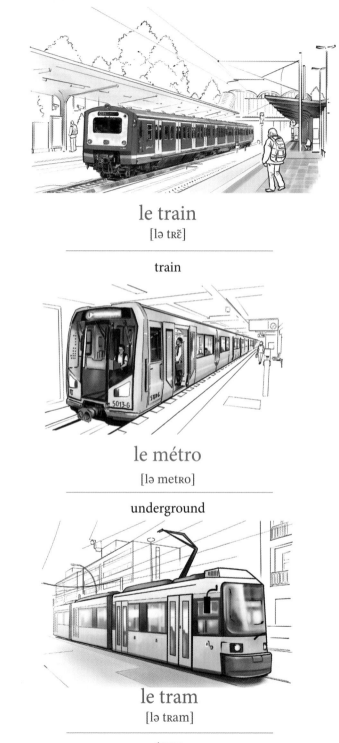

le train
[lə tʁɛ̃]

train

le métro
[lə metʁo]

underground

le tram
[lə tʁam]

tram

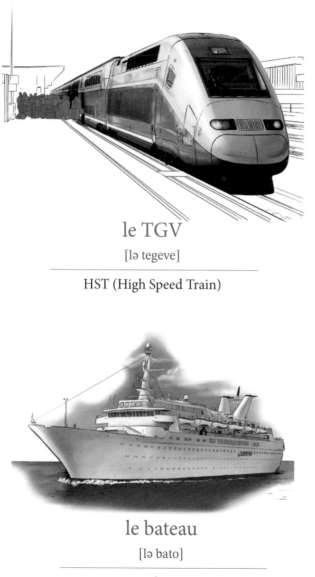

le TGV

[lə tegeve]

HST (High Speed Train)

le bateau

[lə bato]

ship

Accommodation

L'hébergement [lebɛʀʒəmã]

Est-ce que vous avez une chambre
disponible ?

[ɛs‿kə vuz‿ave yn ʃãbʀ dispɔnibl]

Are there any rooms available?

Est-ce que je peux voir la chambre ?

[ɛs‿kə ʒə pø vwaʀ la ʃãbʀ]

May I see the room, please?

Ça coûte combien ?

[sa kut kɔ̃bjɛ̃]

How much is it?

Est-ce que le petit déjeuner est
inclus ?

[ɛs‿kə lə pəti deʒœne ɛ ɛ̃kly]

Is breakfast included?

J'ai réservé une chambre
au nom de ...

[ʒe ʀezɛʀve yn ʃãbʀ o nɔ̃ də]

I have booked a room in
the name of...

Voici ma carte d'identité.

[vwasi ma kaʀt didãtite]

Here is my ID card.

Vous avez le wifi dans votre hôtel ?
[vuz‿ave lə wifi dɑ̃ vɔtʀ‿ɔtɛl]

Do you have Wi-Fi in your hotel?

Est-ce qu'il y a un coffre-fort ?
[ɛs‿kil ja ɛ̃ kɔfʀəfɔʀ]

Is there a safe?

Quand est-ce que je dois libérer
ma chambre ?
[kɑ̃ ɛs‿kə ʒə dwa libeʀe ma ʃɑ̃bʀ]

When do I have to check out?

Est-ce que les réceptionnistes sont
toujours disponibles ?
[ɛs‿kə le ʀesɛpsjɔnist sɔ̃ tuʒuʀ
dispɔnibl]

Is reception open all the time?

Est-ce qu'il y a un restaurant
dans cet hôtel ?
[ɛs‿kil ja ɛ̃ ʀestɔʀɑ̃ dɑ̃ set‿ɔtɛl]

Is there a restaurant in this hotel?

Je voudrais une chambre pour …

[ʒə vudʀɛ yn ʃɑ̃bʀ puʀ]

I would like a room for…

une personne.

[yn pɛʀsɔn]

one person.

deux personnes.

[dø pɛʀsɔn]

two people.

une famille.
[yn famij]

a family.

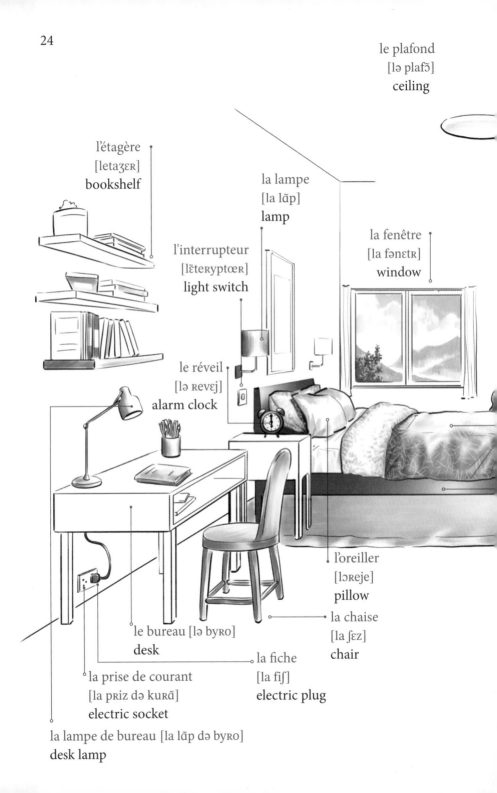

le plafond
[lə plafɔ̃]
ceiling

l'étagère
[letaʒɛʀ]
bookshelf

la lampe
[la lɑ̃p]
lamp

la fenêtre
[la fənɛtʀ]
window

l'interrupteur
[lɛ̃teʀyptœʀ]
light switch

le réveil
[lə ʀevɛj]
alarm clock

l'oreiller
[lɔʀeje]
pillow

la chaise
[la ʃɛz]
chair

le bureau [lə byʀo]
desk

la fiche
[la fiʃ]
electric plug

la prise de courant
[la pʀiz də kuʀɑ̃]
electric socket

la lampe de bureau [la lɑ̃p də byʀo]
desk lamp

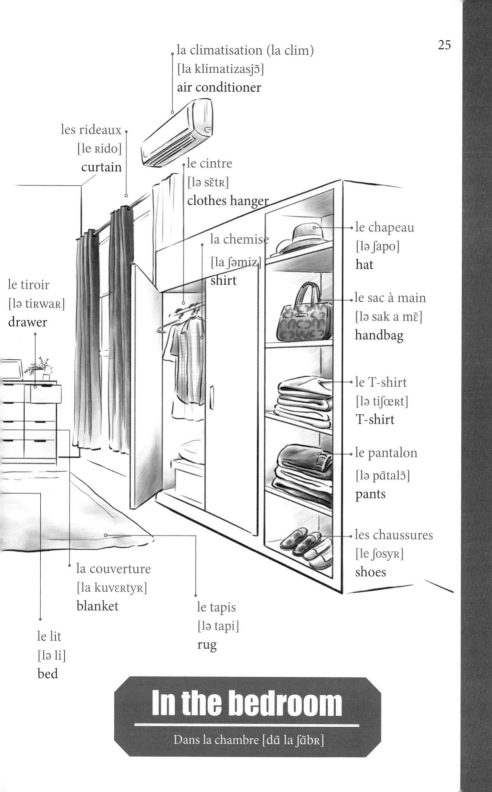

la climatisation (la clim)
[la klimatizasjɔ̃]
air conditioner

les rideaux
[le ʁido]
curtain

le cintre
[lə sɛ̃tʁ]
clothes hanger

la chemise
[la ʃəmiz]
shirt

le chapeau
[lə ʃapo]
hat

le sac à main
[lə sak a mɛ̃]
handbag

le tiroir
[lə tiʁwaʁ]
drawer

le T-shirt
[lə tiʃœʁt]
T-shirt

le pantalon
[lə pɑ̃talɔ̃]
pants

les chaussures
[le ʃosyʁ]
shoes

la couverture
[la kuvɛʁtyʁ]
blanket

le tapis
[lə tapi]
rug

le lit
[lə li]
bed

In the bedroom

Dans la chambre [dɑ̃ la ʃɑ̃bʁ]

In the bathroom

Dans la salle de bains [dɑ̃ la sal də bɛ̃]

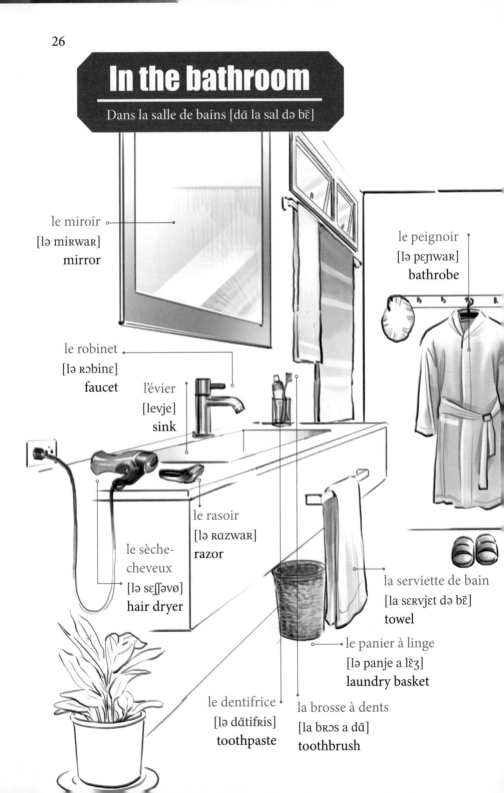

le miroir
[lə miʀwaʀ]
mirror

le peignoir
[lə pɛɲwaʀ]
bathrobe

le robinet
[lə ʀɔbinɛ]
faucet

l'évier
[levje]
sink

le rasoir
[lə ʀɑzwaʀ]
razor

le sèche-
cheveux
[lə sɛʃəvø]
hair dryer

la serviette de bain
[la sɛʀvjɛt də bɛ̃]
towel

le panier à linge
[lə panje a lɛ̃ʒ]
laundry basket

le dentifrice
[lə dɑ̃tifʀis]
toothpaste

la brosse à dents
[la bʀɔs a dɑ̃]
toothbrush

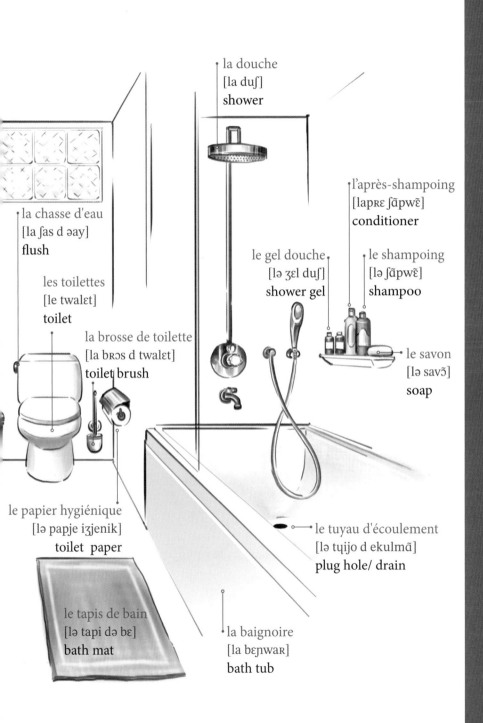

la douche
[la duʃ]
shower

l'après-shampoing
[lapʁɛ ʃɑ̃pwɛ̃]
conditioner

la chasse d'eau
[la ʃas d əay]
flush

le gel douche
[lə ʒɛl duʃ]
shower gel

le shampoing
[lə ʃɑ̃pwɛ̃]
shampoo

les toilettes
[le twalɛt]
toilet

la brosse de toilette
[la bʁɔs d twalɛt]
toilet brush

le savon
[lə savɔ̃]
soap

le papier hygiénique
[lə papje iʒjenik]
toilet paper

le tuyau d'écoulement
[lə tɥijo d ekulmɑ̃]
plug hole/ drain

le tapis de bain
[lə tapi də bɛ]
bath mat

la baignoire
[la bɛɲwaʁ]
bath tub

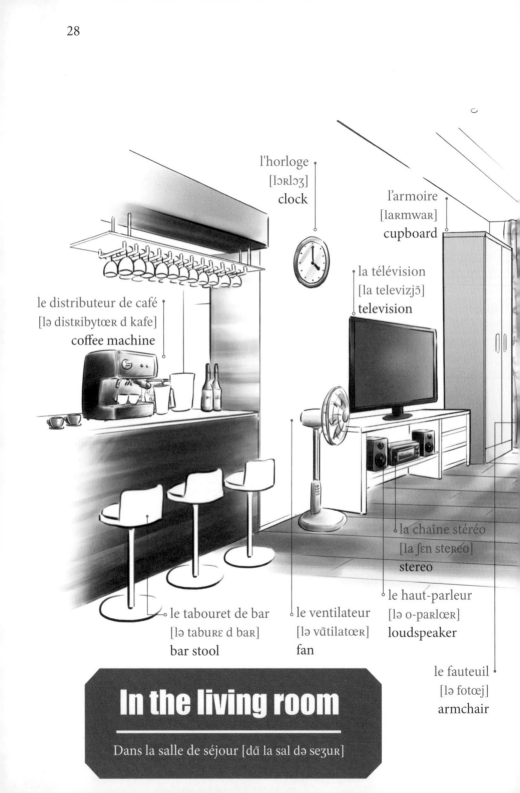

l'horloge
[lɔʀlɔʒ]
clock

l'armoire
[laʀmwaʀ]
cupboard

la télévision
[la televizjɔ̃]
television

le distributeur de café
[lə distʀibytœʀ d kafe]
coffee machine

la chaîne stéréo
[la ʃɛn steʀéo]
stereo

le haut-parleur
[lə o-paʀlœʀ]
loudspeaker

le tabouret de bar
[lə tabuʀɛ d baʀ]
bar stool

le ventilateur
[lə vɑ̃tilatœʀ]
fan

le fauteuil
[lə fotœj]
armchair

In the living room

Dans la salle de séjour [dɑ̃ la sal də seʒuʀ]

la lampe
[la lãp]
light

le piano
[lə pjano]
piano

le tableau
[lə tablo]
picture

les livres
[le livʀ]
books

le violon
[lə vjɔlɔ̃]
violin

le téléphone
[lə telefɔn]
telephone

la table
[la tabl]
table

le vase
[lə vɑz]
vase

le sofa
[lə sɔfa]
sofa

les fleurs
[le flœʀ]
flowers

la télécommande
[la telekɔmãd]
remote control

la poêle
[la pwal]
frying pan

la tasse
[la tɑs]
cup

la bouteille
[la butɛj]
bottle

le verre à vin
[lə vɛʀ a vɛ̃]
wine glass

l'assiette
[lasjɛt]
plate

la cuillère
[la kɥijʀe]
spoon

la fourchette
[la fuʀʃɛt]
fork

la planche
[la plɑ̃ʃ]
chopping board

le robinet
[lə ʀɔbinɛ]
faucet

le micro-ondes
[lə mikʀo-ɔ̃d]
microwave

In the kitchen

Dans la cuisine [dɑ̃ la kɥizin]

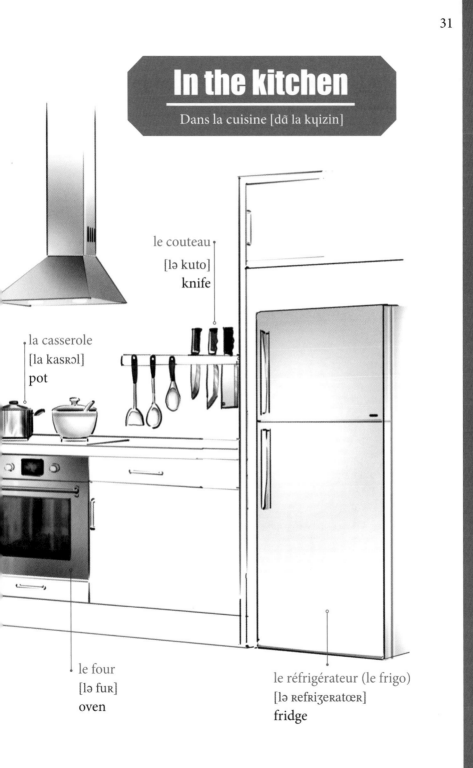

le couteau
[lə kuto]
knife

la casserole
[la kasʀɔl]
pot

le four
[lə fuʀ]
oven

le réfrigérateur (le frigo)
[lə ʀefʀiʒeʀatœʀ]
fridge

Excursions (In the city and in the countryside)

Excursions en ville et à la campagne

[ɛkskyʀsjɔ̃ ɑ̃ vil e a la kɑ̃paɲ]

Quelles sont les attractions touristiques de la région ?

[kɛl sɔ̃ le atʀaksjɔ̃ tuʀistik də la ʀeʒjɔ̃]

What are the tourist attractions in this area?

Où est-ce que je peux goûter les plats locaux ?

[u ɛs‿kəʒ pø gute le pla lɔko]

Where can I try the traditional local food?

Excursions by train

Voyager en train [vwajaʒe ɑ̃ tʀɛ̃]

Où est la gare ?
[u ɛ la gaʀ]

Where is the train station?

Où est le guichet automatique ?
[u ɛ lə giʃɛ otomatik]

Where is the ticket machine?

Où est le guichet ?
[u ɛ lə giʃɛ]

Where is the ticket office?

Combien coûte le bille ?
[kɔ̃bjɛ̃ kut lə bijɛ]

How much does the ticket cost?

Un billet en première classe,
s'il vous plaît.
[ɛ̃ bijɛ ɑ̃ pʀəmjɛʀ klɑs sil vu plɛ]

One first-class ticket, please

Un billet en deuxième classe,
s'il vous plaît.
[ɛ̃ bijɛ ɑ̃ døzjɛm klɑs sil vu plɛ]

One second-class ticket, please.

Un aller simple, s'il vous plaît.
[ɛ̃ ale sɛ̃pl sil vu plɛ]

A one-way ticket, please.

Un billet aller-retour, s'il vous plaît.
[ɛ̃ bijɛ ale ʀətuʀ sil vu plɛ]

A return ticket, please.

Je veux réserver une place.
[ʒ vø ʀezɛʀve yn plas]

I would like to reserve a seat, please.

Quand est-ce que le train
va partir ?
[kɑ̃ ɛs‿kə lə tʀɛ̃ va paʀtiʀ]

What time does the train leave?

Combien de fois est-ce que je dois
changer de train ?
[kɔ̃bjɛ̃ dfwa ɛs‿kə jə dwa ʃɑ̃ʒe də tʀɛ̃]

How many times do I have to
change trains?

Quelle est la prochaine station ?
[kɛl‿e la pʀɔʃɛn stasjɔ̃]

What is the next station called?

Pouvez-vous me dire quand je dois
descendre, s'il vous plaît ?
[puve vu mdiʀ kɑ̃ ʒə dwa
desɑ̃dʀ sil vu plɛ]

Would you please tell me when
I have to get off?

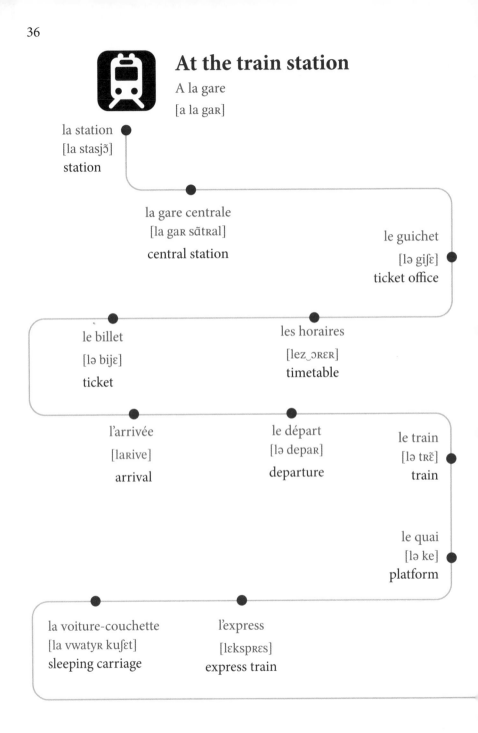

At the train station

A la gare

[a la gaʀ]

la station
[la stasjɔ̃]
station

la gare centrale
[la gaʀ sɑ̃tʀal]
central station

le guichet
[lə giʃɛ]
ticket office

le billet
[lə bijɛ]
ticket

les horaires
[lez ɔʀɛʀ]
timetable

l'arrivée
[laʀive]
arrival

le départ
[lə depaʀ]
departure

le train
[lə tʀɛ̃]
train

le quai
[lə ke]
platform

la voiture-couchette
[la vwatyʀ kuʃɛt]
sleeping carriage

l'express
[lɛkspʀɛs]
express train

le billet de première classe
[lə bijɛ də pʀəmjɛʀ klɑs]
first-class ticket

le billet de deuxième classe
[lə bijɛ də døzjɛm klɑs]
second-class ticket

la réservation de siège
[la ʀezɛʀvasjɔ̃ də sjɛʒ]
seat reservation

un aller-simple
[ɛ̃ ale sɛ̃pl]
one-way

un aller-retour
[ɛ̃ ale ʀətuʀ]
return

la surtaxe
[la syʀtaks]
surcharge

monter
[mɔ̃te]
board

descendre
[desɑ̃dʀ]
get off

changer de train
[ʃɑ̃ʒe də tʀɛ̃]
change trains

A quelle heure est-ce que le train / le bus / le métro / le tram va partir ?

[a kɛl‿œʀ ɛs‿kə lə tʀɛ̃ / lə bys / lə metʀo / lə tʀam va paʀtiʀ]

What time does the train / the bus
the underground / the tram leave?

Excusez-moi,
pouvez-vous m'aider à acheter
un billet avec ce distributeur ?

[ɛkskyze mwa puve vu mede a aʃəte ɛ̃ bijɛ avɛk

sə distribytœʀ]

Excuse me, can you help me to buy
a ticket from the machine?

Je veux aller à ...
[ʒə vø ale a]

I want to go to…

Excursions by bus and tram

Excursions en bus et en tram [ɛkskyʀsjõ ã bys e ã tʀam]

---

l'autobus, le bus [lotobys, lə bys]	bus
l'arrêt de bus [laʀɛ də bys]	bus stop
le tram [lə tʀam]	tram

Où est l'arret de tram ?
[u ɛ laʀɛd tʀam]
Where is the tram stop?

l'arrêt de tram [laʀɛd tʀam]	tram stop
le billet [lə bijɛ]	ticket
le contrôleur lə kõtʀolœʀ]	ticket inspector
l'amende [lamãd]	fine / penalty

Où est ... ?

[u ɛ]

Where is...?

Où est l'arrêt de bus ?

[u ɛ laʁɛd bys]

Where is the bus stop?

le feu rouge

[lə fø ʀuʒ]

traffic lights

la moto

[la moto]

motorcycle

le vélo

[lə velo]

bicycle

la voiture

[la vwatyʀ]

car

Traveling on your own by car, motocycle, bicycle and on foot

Voyager seul en voiture, en moto, à vélo ou à pied

[vwajaʒe sœl ɑ̃ vwatyʀ ɑ̃ mɔto a velo u a pje]

la rue [la ʀy]	street
l'intersection [lɛ̃tɛʀsɛksjɔ̃]	intersection
aller tout droit [ale tu dʀwa]	go straight on
tourner à droite [tuʀne a dʀwat]	turn right
tourner à gauche [tuʀne a goʃ]	turn left
Où est la station d'essence ? [u ɛ la stasjɔ̃ desɑ̃s]	Where is the petrol station?
ici [isi]	here
là [la]	over there
près [pʀɛ]	near
loin [lwɛ̃]	far
l'assurance [lasyʀɑ̃s]	insurance
Quelle essence est-ce que je dois prendre ? [kɛl esɑ̃s ɛs kə ʒə dwa pʀɑ̃dʀ]	What kind of petrol should I put in?

Art amd leisure time activities

Les beaux-arts et les loisirs   [le bozaʀ e le lwaziʀ]

le théâtre
[lə teatʀ]
theater

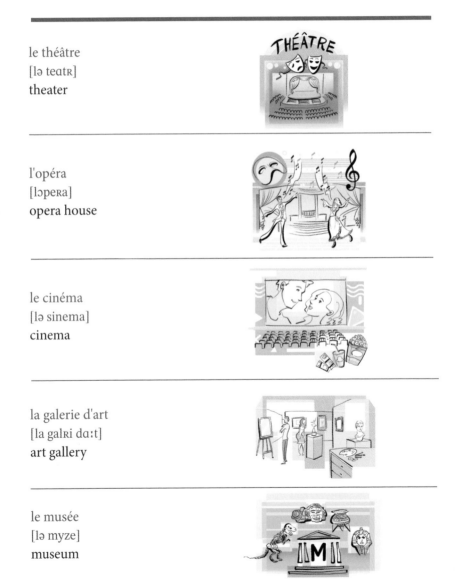

l'opéra
[lɔpeʀa]
opera house

le cinéma
[lə sinema]
cinema

la galerie d'art
[la galʀi dɑːt]
art gallery

le musée
[lə myze]
museum

la piscine
[la pisin]
swimming pool

la piscine extérieure
[la pisin ɛksteʀjœʀ]
outdoor swimming pool

le spa
[lə spa]
spa

le parc municipal
[lə paʀk mynisipal]
city park

la salle de sport
[la sal də spɔʀ]
gym

Tourist attractions

Les sites touristiques [le sit tuʀistik]

la tour Eiffel
[la tuʀ ɛfɛl]
the Eiffel Tower

la cathédrale Notre-Dame
[la katedʀal nɔtʀ-dam]
the Notre-Dame Cathedral

les Champs-Elysées
[le ʃɑ̃selize]
the Champs-Elysees

le musée du Louvre
[lə myze dy luvʀə]
the Louvre museum

le Moulin Rouge
[lə mulɛ̃ ʀuʒ]
the Moulin Rouge

le Panthéon
[lə pɑ̃teõ]
the Pantheon

le pont des Arts
[lə põ de saʀ]
the Pont des Arts

Versailles
[vɛə'saɪ]
The Palace of Versailles

le Sacré-Cœur
[lə sakʀe kœʀ]
the Sacred Heart

le centre Pompidou
[lə sɑ̃tʀ põpidu]
the Centre Pompidou

At the bakery

Boulangerie [bulɑ̃ʒʀi]

la baguette
[la bagɛt]

baguette

le pain au noix
[lə pɛ o nwa]

walnut bread

le croissant
[lə kʀwasɑ̃]

croissant

le pain de campagne
[lə pɛ̃ də kɑ̃paɲ]

country bread

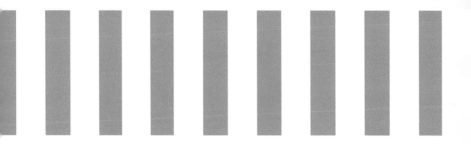

le pain bâtard
[lə pɛ̃ bataʀ]

"bâtard" bread

la fougasse
[la fugas]

fougasse

le pain complet
[lə pɛ̃ kɔ̃plɛ]

wholemeal bread

la brioche
[la bʀijɔʃ]

brioche

l'agneau
[laɲo]
lamb

le lapin
[lə lapɛ̃]
rabbit

le canard
[lə kanaʁ]
duck

le bœuf
[lə bœf]
beef

le veau
[lə vo]
veal

At the butchers

Dans la boucherie [dɑ̃ la buʃʀi]

le porc
[lə pɔʀ]
pork

les viandes
[le vjɑ̃d]
meats

l'escargot
[lɛskaʀgo]
snail

le poulet
[lə pulɛ]
chicken

At the fishmonger

Dans la poissonnerie [dã la pwasɔnʀi]

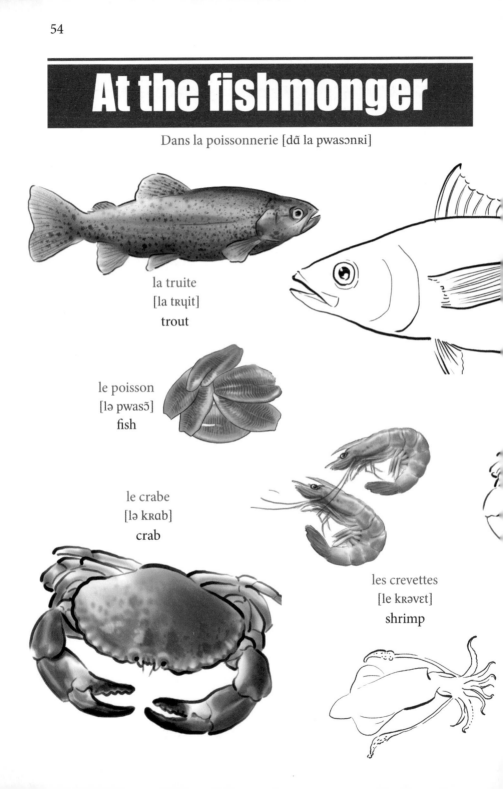

la truite
[la tʀɥit]
trout

le poisson
[lə pwasɔ̃]
fish

le crabe
[lə kʀab]
crab

les crevettes
[le kʀəvɛt]
shrimp

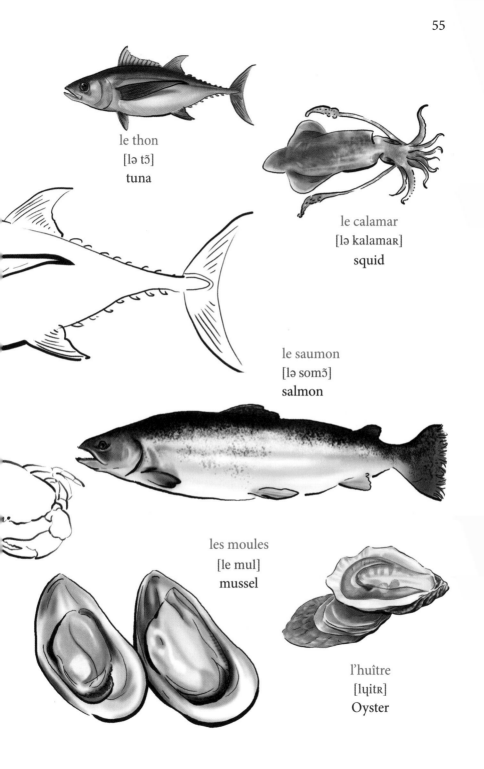

le thon
[lə tɔ̃]
tuna

le calamar
[lə kalamaʀ]
squid

le saumon
[lə somɔ̃]
salmon

les moules
[le mul]
mussel

l'huître
[lɥitʀ]
Oyster

1

2

3

4

5

6

7

8

9

In the vegetable shop

Au rayon légumes [o ʀɛjɔ̃ legym]

1. l'aubergine [lobɛʀʒin]
aubergine

2. le concombre [lə kɔ̃kɔ̃bʀ]
cucumber

3. le brocoli [lə bʀɔkɔli]
broccoli

4. l'artichaut [laʀtiʃo]
artichoke

5. le chou chinois [lə ʃu ʃinwa]
Chinese cabbage

6. les petits pois [le pəti pwɑ]
peas

7. le chou-fleur [lə ʃuflœʀ]
cauliflower

8. les carottes [le kaʀɔt]
carrots

9. le basilic [lə bazilik]
basil

1. le gingembre [lə ʒɛ̃ʒɑ̃bʀ]
   ginger

2. la laitue [la lety]
   lettuce

3. la citrouille [la sitʀuj]
   pumpkin

4. les amandes [lez‿amɑ̃d]
   almonds

5. les cacahouètes [le kakaɥɛt]
   peanuts

6. les noisettes [le nwazɛt]
   hazelnuts

7. l'ail [laj]
   garlic

8. les champignons [le ʃɑ̃piɲɔ̃]
   mushrooms

9. les pommes de terre [le pɔm də tɛʀ]
   potatoes

10. le maïs [lə mais]
    corn

11. les noix [le nwa]
    walnuts

1

2

3

4

7

5

6

8

9

10

11

1. la betterave [la bɛtʀav]
   beetroot

2. le poivron [lə pwavʀɔ̃]
   bell pepper

3. l'oignon [lɔɲɔ̃]
   onion

4. le chou blanc [lə ʃu blɑ̃]
   white cabbage

5. le chou rouge [lə ʃu ʀuʒ]
   red cabbage

6. l'asperge [laspɛʀʒ]
   asparagus

7. la tomate [la tɔmat]
   tomato

8. la courgette [la kuʀʒɛt]
   courgette

9. le céleri [lə sɛlʀi]
   celery

10. les épinards [lez‿epinaʀ]
    spinach

la pomme	la pomme verte	la poire
[la pɔm]	[la pɔm vɛʀt]	[la pwaʀ]
apple	green apple	pear

la cerise	la prune	l'olive
[la səʀiz]	[la pʀyn]	[lɔliv]
cherry	plum	olive

la noix de coco	la fraise	l'ananas
[la nwad koko]	[la fʀɛz]	[lanana]
coconut	strawberry	pineapple

la grenade
[la gʀənad]
pomegranate

la mûre
[la myʀ]
blackberry

la framboise
[la fʀɑ̃bwaz]
raspberry

In the fruit shop

Au rayon fruits [o ʀɛjõ fʀɥi]

la myrtille
[la miʀtij]
blueberry

le cassis
[lə kasis]
blackcurrant

la groseille
[la gʀozɛj]
redcurrant

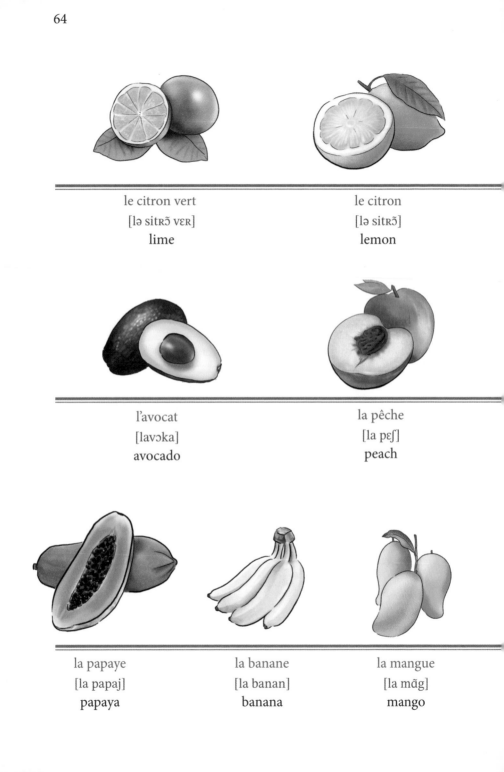

le citron vert
[lə sitʁɔ̃ vɛʁ]
lime

le citron
[lə sitʁɔ̃]
lemon

l'avocat
[lavɔka]
avocado

la pêche
[la pɛʃ]
peach

la papaye
[la papaj]
papaya

la banane
[la banan]
banana

la mangue
[la mɑ̃g]
mango

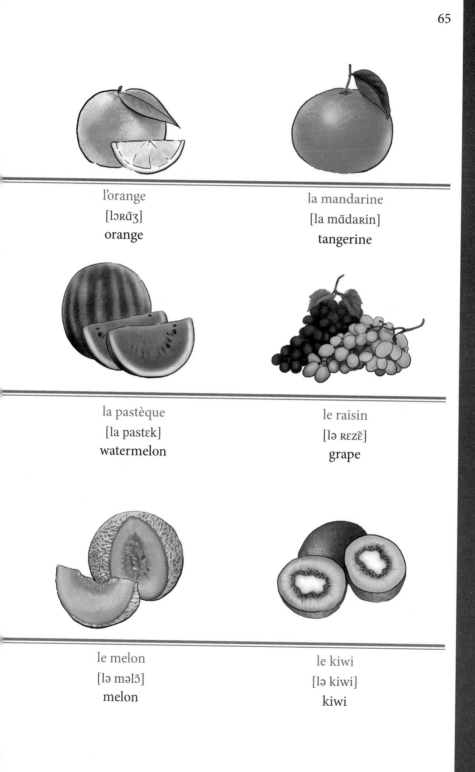

l'orange
[lɔʀɑ̃ʒ]
orange

la mandarine
[la mɑ̃daʀin]
tangerine

la pastèque
[la pastɛk]
watermelon

le raisin
[lə ʀɛzɛ̃]
grape

le melon
[lə məlɔ̃]
melon

le kiwi
[lə kiwi]
kiwi

Beverages

les boissons [le bwasɔ̃]

l'eau pétillante
[lo petijɑ̃t]
sparkling water

l'eau plate
[lo pla]
still water

l'eau minérale
[lo mineʀal]
mineral water

la limonade
[la limɔnad]
lemon soda

les boissons gazeuses
[le bwasɔ̃ gazøs]
soda

le jus de carotte
[lə ʒyd kaʁɔt]
carrot juice

le jus d'ananas
[lə ʒy danana]
pineapple juice

le jus de pomme
[lə ʒyd pɔm]
apple juice

le jus de tomate
[lə ʒyd tɔmat]
tomato juice

le jus d'orange
[lə ʒy dɔʁɑ̃ʒ]
orange juice

le jus de raisin
[lə ʒyd ʁɛzɛ̃]
grape juice

At the Bar

Dans le bar [dã lə baʀ]

la bière
[la bjɛʀ]
beer

le vin mousseux
[lə vɛ̃ musø]
sparkling wine

le whiskey
[lə wiski]
whisky

le cognac
[lə kɔɲak]
brandy

le vin rouge
[lə vɛ̃ ʀuʒ]
red wine

le vin blanc
[lə vɛ̃ blɑ̃ʃ]
white wine

le rosé
[lə ʀoze]
rosé wine

La vérité est dans le vin.
[la veʀite ɛ dã lə vɛ̃] The truth is in the wine.

Le vin est de la poésie en bouteille.
[lə vɛ̃ ɛ də la pɔezi ã butɛj] Wine is poetry in a bottle.

Le vin blanc rend aussi le nez rouge.
[lə vɛ̃ blã ʀã osi lə ne ʀuʒ] White wine can also make your nose red.

La vie
est
trop courte
pour boire
du mauvais
Vin.

[la vi ɛ tʀo kuʀt puʀ bwaʀ dy mɔvɛ vɛ̃]

Life is too short to drink bad wine.

Johann Wolfgang von Goethe

le café express
[lə kafe ɛkspʀɛs]

le café noisette
[lə kafe nwazɛt]

le café allongé
[lə kafe alõʒe]

At the coffee shop

Au Café [o kafe]

le café express

espresso

le café noisette

espresso with whipped hot milk foam

le café allongé

espresso with hot water

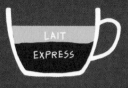

le café crème
[lə kafe kʁɛm]

le chocolat chaud
[lə ʃɔkɔla ʃod]

le lait chaud
[lə lɛ ʃod]

le café crème

white coffee

le chocolat chaud

hot chocolate

le lait chaud

hot milk

Tea

le thé [lə te]

1. le thé noir
[lə te nwaʀ]
black tea

2. le thé blanc
[lə te blɑ̃]
white tea

3. le thé vert
[lə te vɛʀ]
green tea

4. le thé aux fruits
[lə te o fʀɥi]
fruit tea

5. le thé jaune
[lə te ʒon]
yellow tea

6. la tisane
[la tizan]
herbal tea

Excusez-moi, je voudrais commander.

[ɛkskyze mwa ʒə vudʀɛ kɔmɑ̃de]

Excuse me, I would like to order, please.

Quelle sont les spécialités
de cette région ?

[kɛl sɔ̃ le spesjalite də sɛt ʀeʒjɔ̃]

What are the specialties of this region?

In the restaurant

Dans le restaurant [dã lə RɛstɔRã]

le restaurant [lə RɛstɔRã] restaurant

le menu [lə məny] menu

l'entrée [lãtRe] starter

le plat principal [lə pla pRɛ̃sipal] main course

le dessert [lə desɛR] dessert

Est-ce que vous avez une table
pour deux personnes ?
[ɛs‿kə vuz‿ave yn tabl puR dø pɛRsɔn]

Do you have a table for two?

Vous avez un plat du jour ?
[vuz‿ave ɛ̃ pla dy ʒuR]

What is today's special?

Qu'est-ce que vous
me recommandez ?
[kɛs kə vum Rəkɔmãde]

What would you recommend?

Je voudrais …
[ʒə vudRɛ]

I would like…

1. la fourchette à salade [la fuʁʃɛt a salad]
   salad fork

2. la fourchette [la fuʁʃɛt]
   dinner fork

3. le couteau [lə kuto]
   dinner knife

4. le couteau à salade [lə kuto a salad]
   salad knife

5. la cuillère à soupe [la kɥijʁe a sup]
   soup spoon

6. le couteau à beurre [la kɥijʁe a bœr]
   butter knife

7. la fourchette à dessert [la fuʁʃɛt a desɛʁ]
   dessert fork

8. la cuillère à dessert [la kɥijʁe a desɛʁ]
   dessert spoon

9. l'assiette à pain [lasjɛt a pɛ̃]
   bread plate

10. la sous-assiette [la suz‿asjɛt]
    main plate

11. le verre à eau [lə vɛʁ a o]
    water glass

12. le verre à vin rouge [lə vɛʁ a vɛ̃ ʁuʒ]
    red wine glass

13. le verre à vin blanc [lə vɛʁ a vɛ̃ blɑ̃]
    white wine glass

Formal table setting

Les couverts de table [le kuvɛʁ də tabl]

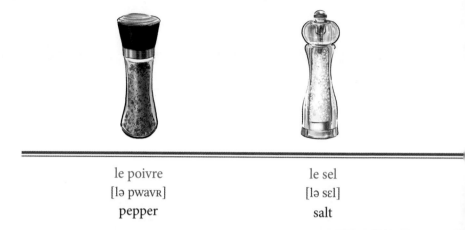

le poivre	le sel
[lə pwavʀ]	[lə sɛl]
pepper	salt

Seasonings

L'assaisonnements [lasɛzɔnmɑ̃]

le piment	le pistou	le curry
[lə pimɑ̃]	[lə pistu]	[lə kyʀi]
chili powder	pesto	curry powder

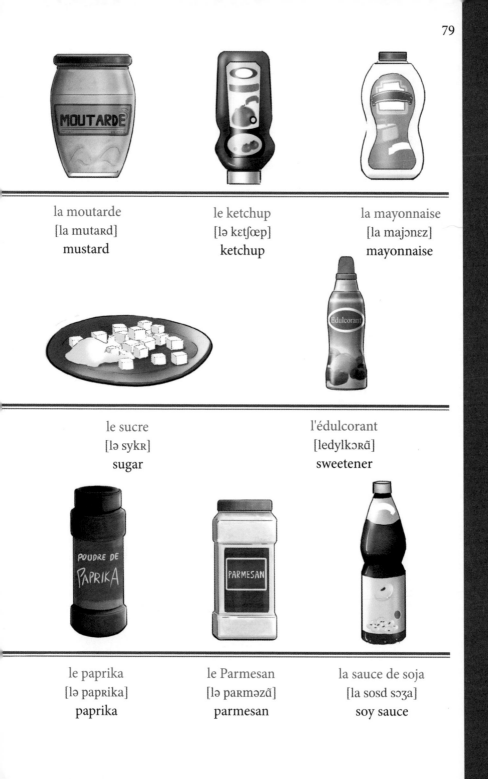

la moutarde
[la mutaʀd]
mustard

le ketchup
[lə kɛtʃœp]
ketchup

la mayonnaise
[la majɔnɛz]
mayonnaise

le sucre
[lə sykʀ]
sugar

l'édulcorant
[ledylkɔʀɑ̃]
sweetener

le paprika
[lə papʀika]
paprika

le Parmesan
[lə paʀməzɑ̃]
parmesan

la sauce de soja
[la sosd sɔʒa]
soy sauce

le repas	[lə ʀəpɑ]	meal
le petit déjeuner	[lə pəti deʒœne]	breakfast
le déjeuner	[lə deʒœne]	lunch
le dîner	[lə dine]	dinner

Bon appétit !

[bɔ̃n_apeti]

Enjoy your meal!

L'addition, s'il vous plaît.

[ladisjɔ̃ sil vu plɛ]

May I have the bill, please?

Le repas était très bon !
[lə ʀəpɑ etɛ tʀɛ bɔ̃]

The food was very good!

Délicieux !
[delisjø]

Delicious!

C'est bien comme ça.
[sɛ bjɛ̃ kɔm sa]

Keep the change.

le pourboire
[lə puʀbwaʀ]

tip

la confiture
[la kɔ̃fityʀ]
jam

le miel
[lə mjɛl]
honey

le beurre de cacahouète
[lə bœʀ də kakauɛt]
peanut butter

le beurre
[lə bœʀ]
butter

le fromage
[lə fʀɔmaʒ]
cheese

le toast
[lə tost]
toast

l'œuf à la coque
[lœf a la kɔk]
soft-boiled egg

l'omelette
[lɔmlɛt]
omelet

Breakfast

Le petit déjeuner [lə pəti dezœne]

le muesli
[lə mysli]
muesli

la salade de fruits
[la salad də fʁɥi]
fruit salad

le yaourt
[lə jauʁ]
yogurt

l'œuf au plat
[lœf o pla]
fried egg

le jambon
[lə ʒɑ̃bɔ̃]
ham

les œufs brouillés
[lez‿œf bʁuje]
scrambled eggs

Starter

L'entrée [lɑ̃tʀe]

les crudités

[le kʀydite]

crudités

les canapés

[le kanape]

canapés

le foie gras

[lə fwa gʀɑ]

foie gras

les huîtres

[le ɥitʀ]

oysters

Main course

Le plat principal [lə pla pʀɛ̃sipal]

le coq au vin
[lə kɔk‿o vɛ̃]
coq au vin

la bouillabaisse
[la bujabɛs]
bouillabaisse fish stew

le poulet rôti et pommes de terre
[lə pulɛ ʀoti e pɔm dtɛʀ]
roast chicken and potatoes

les paupiettes de veau rôties
[le popjɛt dvo ʀoti]
roasted veal paupiettes

les moules marinières
[le mul maʀinjɛʀ]
mussels in white wine sauce

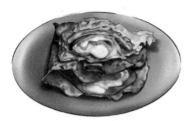

la crêpe jambon-fromage
[la kʀɛp ʒɑ̄bɔ̃ fʀɔmaʒ]
ham and cheese crepe

la poêlée d'escargots aux girolles
[la pwale dɛskaʀgo o ʒiʀɔl]
fried snails with chanterelle mushrooms

la petite choucroute de la mer
[la pəti ʃukʀut də la mɛʀ]
seafood with sauerkraut

le cassoulet
[lə kasulɛ]
cassoulet

le gratin dauphinois
[lə gʀatɛ̃ dofinwa]
potato gratin

Snacks

Le snack [lə snak]

le hamburger
[lə ãbuʀɡœʀ]
hamburger

le sandwich
[lə sãdwiʃ]
sandwich

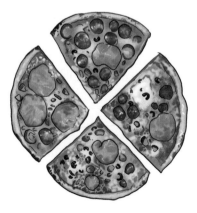

la pizza
[la pidza]
pizza

Dessert

Le dessert [lə desɛʀ]

---

1. la crêpe [la kʀɛp] crêpe

• • •

2. la crème brûlée [la kʀɛm bʀyle] crème brûlée

• • •

3. la meringue [la məʀɛ̃g] meringue

• • •

4. le chou à la crème [lə ʃu ɑ̃ la kʀɛm] cream puff

• • •

5. la tarte aux pommes [la taʀt‿o pɔm] apple pie

• • •

6. le macaron [la makaʀɔ̃] macaron

• • •

7. le gâteau roulé [lə gɑto ʀule] roll cake

• • •

8. le mille-feuille [lə milfœj] mille-feuille pastry

• • •

9. l'éclair [leklɛʀ] éclair

• • •

10. le nid d'abeille [lə ni dabɛj] nid d'abeille

• • •

11. la tarte au citron [la taʀt‿o sitʀɔ̃] lemon pie

Cheeses

Les fromages [le fʀɔmaʒ]

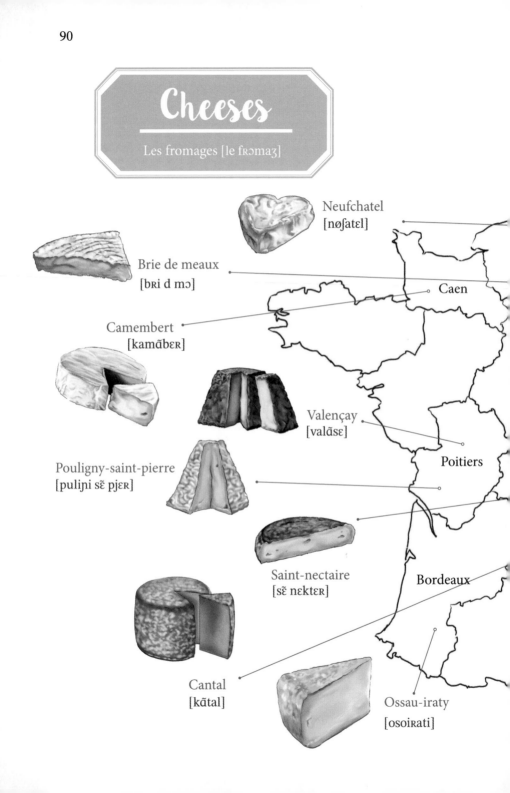

Neufchatel
[nøʃatɛl]

Brie de meaux
[bʀi d mɔ]

Caen

Camembert
[kamɑ̃bɛʀ]

Valençay
[valɑ̃sɛ]

Poitiers

Pouligny-saint-pierre
[puliɲi sɛ̃ pjɛʀ]

Saint-nectaire
[sɛ̃ nɛktɛʀ]

Bordeaux

Cantal
[kɑ̃tal]

Ossau-iraty
[osoiʀati]

Chaource
[ʃauʀs]

Langres
[lãgʀ]

Munster gerome
[mœ̃stɛʀ ʒəʀɔm]

Amiens

Comté
[kɔ̃te]

Paris

Strasbourg

Reblochon
[ʀəblɔʃɔ̃]

Dijons

Besançon

Beaufort
[bofɔʀ]

Lyon

Clermont
Ferrand

Roquefort
[ʀɔkfɔʀ]

Mont-
pellier

Marseille

Banon
[banɔ̃]

Bleu des Caussses
[blœ de kos]

Pélardon
[pelaʀdɔ̃]

Places to shop

Faire du shopping [fɛʀ dy ʃɔpiŋ]

Monoprix

Fnac

Intermarché

Carrefour

Auchan

le centre commercial
[lə sɑ̃tʀ kɔmɛʀsjal]
shopping mall

le supermarché
[lə sypɛʀmaʀʃe]
supermarket

l'hypermarché
[lipɛʀmaʀʃe]
hypermarket

le magasin
[lə magazɛ̃]
shop

l'épicerie
[lepisʀĩ]
grocery store

Everything your heart desires

Tout ce que vous désirez [tu sə kə vu deziʀe]

la parfumerie
[la paʀfymʀi]
cosmetic shop

le coiffeur
[lə kwafœʀ]
hair salon

le bijoutier
[lə biʒutje]
jewellery shop

le fleuriste
[lə flœʀist]
flower shop

la boutique de mode
[la butik də mɔd]
fashion boutique

le magasin de chaussures
[lə magazɛ̃ də ʃosyʀ]
shoe shop

le magasin de souvenirs
[lə magazɛ̃ də suvəniʀ]
souvenir shop

l'antiquaire
[lɑ̃tikɛʀ]
antique shop

Je cherche …

I would like…

[ʒə ʃɛRʃ]

une chemise.

a shirt.

[yn ʃəmiz]

un pantalon.

a pair of trousers.

[ɛ̃ pɑ̃talɔ̃]

une paire de chaussures.

a pair of shoes.

[yn pɛR də ʃosyR]

une paire de chausettes.

a pair of socks.

[yn pɛR də ʃosɛt]

deux chemisiers.

two blouses.

[dø ʃəmizje]

trois vestes.

three jackets.

[tRwɑ vɛst]

quatre robes.

four dresses.

[katR Rɔb]

cinq manteaux.

five coats.

[sɛ̃k mɑ̃to]

Ça coûte combien ?
[sa kut kɔ̃bjɛ̃]

How much does it cost?

Ça coûte …. euros.
[sa kut øʀos]

It costs ... euro.

C'est très cher.
[sɛ tʀɛ ʃɛʀ]

That is very expensive.

Pouvez vous me faire
une réduction ?
[puve vu mə fɛʀ yn ʀedyksjɔ̃]

Can you give me a better price?

C'est très bon marché.
[sɛ tʀɛ bɔ̃ maʀʃe]

That is very cheap.

Merci, c'est tout.
[mɛʀsi sɛ tu]

That's everything, thanks.

Le prix est raisonnable.
[lə pʀi ɛ ʀɛzɔnabl]

The price is reasonable.

C'est trop court / trop long.
[sɛ tʀo kuʀ / tʀo lɔ̃]

It's too short / too long.

C'est trop large / trop serré.
[sɛ tʀo laʀʒ / tʀo seʀe]

It's too big / too tight.

Est-ce que je peux essayer ?

[ɛs_kə ʒpø eseje]

May I try it on?

Où sont les cabines d'essayage ?

[u sɔ̃ le kabin deseja ʒ]

Where is the fitting room?

En solde

[ɑ̃ sɔld]

On sale

En promotion
[ɑ̃ pʀɔmosjɔ̃] on promotion

Offre spéciale
[ɔfʀ spesjal] special offer

A prix réduit
[a pʀi ʀedɥi] at a reduced price

Colors

Les couleurs [le kulœʀ]

blanc, blanche
[blɑ̃, blɑ̃ʃ]
white

noir, noire
[nwaʀ]
black

orange
[ɔʀɑ̃ʒ]
orange

marron
[maʀɔ̃]
brown

gris, grise
[gʀi, gʀiz]
gray

bleu, bleue
[blø]
blue

clair(e)
[klɛʀ]
light

foncé(e)
[fɔ̃se]
dark

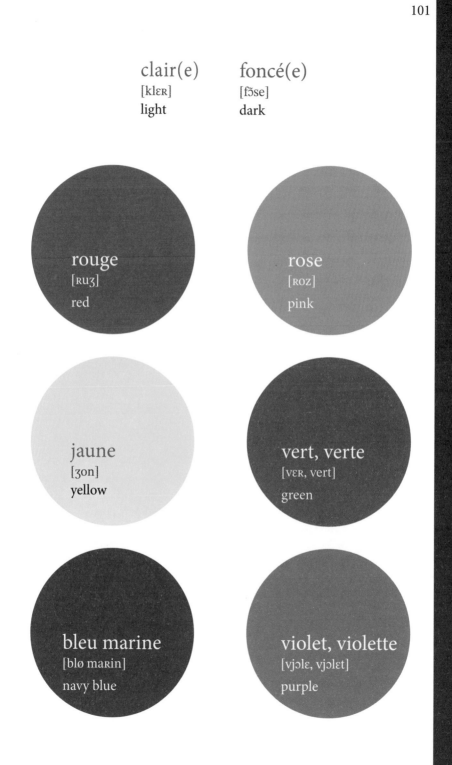

rouge
[ʀuʒ]
red

rose
[ʀoz]
pink

jaune
[ʒon]
yellow

vert, verte
[vɛʀ, vɛʀt]
green

bleu marine
[blø maʀin]
navy blue

violet, violette
[vjɔlɛ, vjɔlɛt]
purple

Numbers

Les nombres [le nɔ̃bʀ]

0	zéro	[zeʀo]
1	un	[ɛ̃]
2	deux	[dø]
3	trois	[tʀwɑ]
4	quatre	[katʀ]
5	cinq	[sɛ̃k]
6	six	[sis]
7	sept	[sɛt]
8	huit	[ɥit]
9	neuf	[nœf]
10	dix	[dis]
11	onze	[ɔ̃z]
12	douze	[duz]
13	treize	[tʀɛz]
14	quatorze	[katɔʀz]
15	quinze	[kɛ̃z]
16	seize	[sɛz]
17	dix-sept	[disɛt]
18	dix-huit	[dizɥit]
19	dix-neuf	[diznœf]
20	vingt	[vɛ̃]
21	vingt et un	[vɛ̃t‿e ɛ̃]
22	vingt-deux	[vɛ̃ dø]
23	vingt-trois	[vɛ̃ tʀwɑ]
24	vingt-quatre	[vɛ̃ katʀ]
25	vingt-cinq	[vɛ̃ sɛ̃k]

26	vingt-six	[vɛ̃ sis]
27	vingt-sept	[vɛ̃ sɛt]
28	vingt-huit	[vɛ̃ ɥit]
29	vingt-neuf	[vɛ̃ nœf]
30	trente	[tʀɑ̃t]
40	quarante	[kaʀɑ̃t]
50	cinquante	[sɛ̃kɑ̃t]
60	soixante	[swasɑ̃t]
70	soixante-dix	[swasɑ̃t dis]
80	quatre-vingt	[katʀ vɛ̃]
90	quatre-vingt-dix	[katʀ vɛ̃ dis]
100	cent	[sɑ̃]
101	cent un	[sɑ̃ ɛ̃]
102	cent deux	[sɑ̃ dø]
200	deux cents	[dø sɑ̃]
300	trois cents	[tʀwɑ sɑ̃]
400	quatre cents	[katʀ sɑ̃]
500	cinq cents	[sɛ̃k sɑ̃]
600	six cents	[si sɑ̃]
700	sept cents	[sɛt sɑ̃]
800	huit cents	[ɥit sɑ̃]
900	neuf cents	[nœf sɑ̃]
1000	mille	[mil]
10 000	dix mille	[di mil]
100 000	cent mille	[sɑ̃ mil]
1 000 000	un million	[ɛ̃ miljɔ̃]

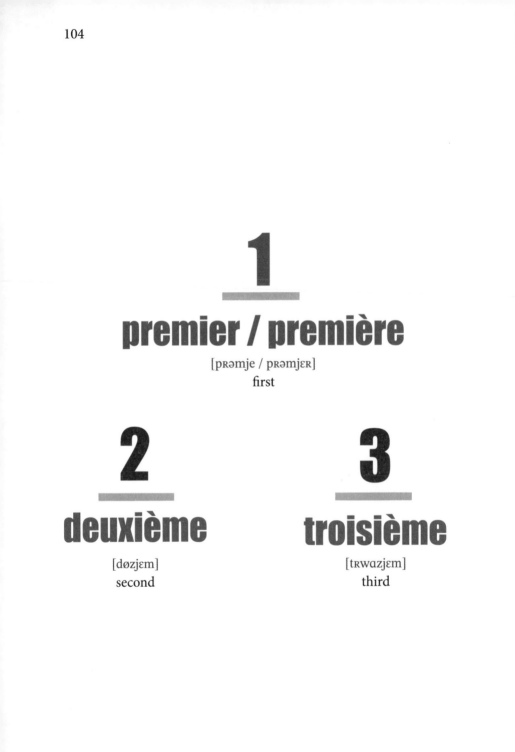

1

premier / première

[pʀəmje / pʀəmjɛʀ]

first

2

deuxième

[døzjɛm]

second

3

troisième

[tʀwazjɛm]

third

quatrième	[katʀijɛm]	fourth
cinquième	[sɛ̃kjɛm]	fifth
sixième	[sizjɛm]	sixth
septième	[sɛtjɛm]	seventh
huitième	[ɥitjɛm]	eighth
neuvième	[nœvjɛm]	ninth
dixième	[dizjɛm]	tenth

When then?

Quand donc? [kɑ̃ dõk]

hier

[jɛʀ]

yesterday

hier soir

[jɛʀ swaʀ]

yesterday evening

avant-hier

[avɑ̃t jɛʀ]

the day before yesterday

la semaine dernière

[la səmɛn dɛʀnjɛʀ]

last week

l'année dernière

[lane dɛʀnjɛʀ]

last year

aujourd'hui
[oʒuʀdɥi]

today

demain
[dəmɛ̃]

tomorrow

après-demain
[apʀɛ dəmɛ̃]

the day after tomorrow

la semaine prochaine
[la səmɛn pʀɔʃɛn]

next week

l'année prochaine
[lane pʀɔʃɛn]

next year

110

All about time

A propos de l'heure [a pʀɔpo də lœʀ]

le temps	[lə tã]	time
l'horloge	[lɔʀlɔʒ]	clock
la seconde	[la səgɔ̃d]	second
les secondes	[le səgɔ̃d]	seconds
la minute	[la minyt]	minute
les minutes	[le minyt]	minutes
un quart d'heure	[yn kaʀ dœʀ]	quarter of an hour
une demi-heure	[yn dəmi œʀ]	half an hour
l'heure	lœʀ]	hour
les heures	[lez‿œʀ]	hours

le matin	le midi	l'après-midi	la soirée
[lə matɛ̃]	[lə midi]	[lapʀɛ-midi]	[la swaʀe]
morning	noon	afternoon	evening

la nuit	minuit
[la nɥi]	[minɥi]
night	midnight

tôt
[to]
early

tard
[taʀ]
late

Quelle heure est-il ?

[kɛl‿œr ɛt‿il]

What time is it?

7:10
Il est sept heures dix.
[il‿ɛ sɛt‿œr dis]
It's ten past seven.

Il est une heure.

[il ɛ yn œʀ]

It's one a.m.

7:15

Il est sept heures et quart.

[il ɛ sɛt œʀ e kaʀ]

It's a quarter past seven.

8:00

Il est huit heures.

[il ɛ ɥit œʀ]

It's eight a.m.

7: 55

Il est sept heures cinquante cinq.

[il ɛ sɛt œʀ sɛ̃kɑ̃t sɛk]

It's five to eight.

9:50

Il est neuf heures cinquante.

[il ɛ nœf œʀ sɛ̃kɑ̃t]

It's ten to ten.

10:00

Il est dix heures.

[il ɛ diz œʀ]

It's ten a.m.

10:10

Il est dix heures dix.

[il ɛ diz œʀ dis]

It's ten past ten.

10:30
dix heures et demi.
[il ɛ diz œʀ e dəmi]
It's half past ten.

12:00
Il est midi.
[il ɛ midi]
It's midday.

17:45
Il est dix-sept heures quarante-cinq.
[il ɛ dissɛt œʀ kaʀɑ̃tsɛ̃k]
It's a quarter to six.

20:00
Il est vingt heures.
[il ɛ vɛ̃t œʀ]
It's eight p.m.

Seven days of the week

Les sept jours de la semaine
[le sɛt ʒuʀ də la səmɛn]

dimanche	**lundi**	**mardi**
[dimɑ̃ʃ]	[lɛ̃di]	[maʀdi]
Sunday	Monday	Tuesday

le jour de travail   work day
[le ʒuʀ də tʀavaj]

le weekend   weekend
[lə wikɛnd]

le jour férié   public holiday
[lə ʒuʀ feʀje]

le jour de repos   day off
[lə ʒuʀ də ʀəpo]

mercredi	**jeudi**	**vendredi**	**samedi**
[mɛʀkʀədi]	[ʒødi]	[vɑ̃dʀədi]	[samdi]
Wednesday	Thursday	Friday	Saturday

Quel jour sommes-nous ?
[kɛl ʒuʀ sɔmnu]

What day is it today?

Nous sommes lundi.
[nu sɔm lɛ̃di]

It's Monday.

On est quelle date d'aujourd'hui ?
[ɔ̃n ɛ kɛl dat doʒuʀdɥi]

What date is it today?

On est le 10 janvier.
[ɔ̃n ɛ lə dis ʒɑ̃vje]

It's January 10th.

Est-ce que c'est un jour férié
aujourd'hui ?
[ɛs kə sɛ ɛ̃ ʒuʀ feʀje oʒuʀdɥi]

Is today a public holiday?

1
Janvier
[ʒɑ̃vje]
January

2
Février
[fevʀije]
February

5
Mai
[mɛ]
May

6
Juin
[ʒɥɛ̃]
June

9
Septembre
[sɛptɑ̃bʀ]
September

10
Octobre
[ɔktɔbʀ]
October

The twelves months of the year

Les douze mois de l'année [le duz mwa də lane]

3

Mars

[maʀs]

March

4

Avril

[avʀil]

April

7

Juillet

[ʒɥijɛ]

July

8

Août

[ut]

August

11

Novembre

[nɔvɑ̃bʀ]

November

12

Décembre

[desɑ̃bʀ]

December

The weather and seasons

La météo et les saisons [la meteo e le sɛzɔ̃]

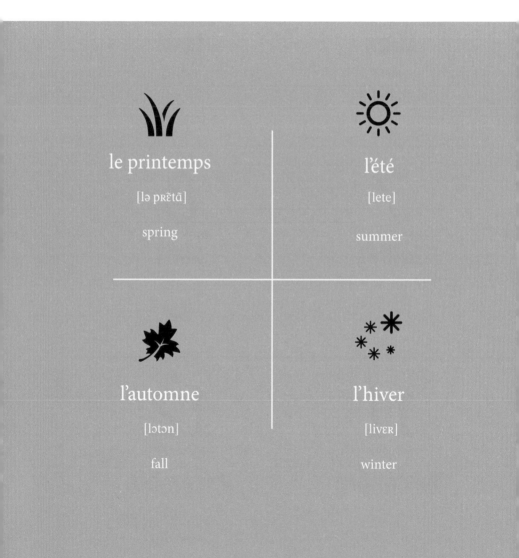

le printemps

[lə pʀɛ̃tɑ̃]

spring

l'été

[lete]

summer

l'automne

[lɔtɔn]

fall

l'hiver

[livɛʀ]

winter

Quel temps fait-il aujourd'hui ? What's the weather like today?
[kɛl tɑ̃ fɛt‿il oʒuʀdɥi]

Il fait beau aujourd'hui. The weather is fine today.
[il fɛ bo oʒuʀdɥi]

Il y a du soleil. It's sunny.
[il‿ja dy sɔlɛj]

Il fait mauvais aujourd'hui. The weather is bad today.
[il fɛ mɔvɛ oʒuʀdɥi]

Il fait chaud. It's hot.
[il fɛ ʃo]

Il fait très chaud. It's very hot.
[il fɛ tʀɛ ʃo]

J'ai très chaud. I'm boiling.
[ʒɛ tʀɛ ʃo]

Il fait très froid. It's really cold.
[il fɛ tʀɛ fʀwa]

J'ai très froid. I'm freezing.
[ʒɛ tʀɛ fʀwa]

Il y a beaucoup de vent. It's windy.
[il‿ja boku də vɑ̃]

Il y a du brouillard. It's foggy.
[il‿ja dy bʀujaʀ]

Il pleut. It's rainy.
[il plø]

Il bruine. It's drizzling.
[il bʀɥin]

Il neige. It's snowing.
[il nɛʒ]

le front
[lə fʀɔ̃] forehead

l'œil
[lœj] eye

le nez
[lə ne] nose

la bouche
[la buʃ] mouth

les dents
[le dɑ̃] teeth

la langue
[la lɑ̃g] tongue

le menton
[lə mɑ̃tɔ̃] chin

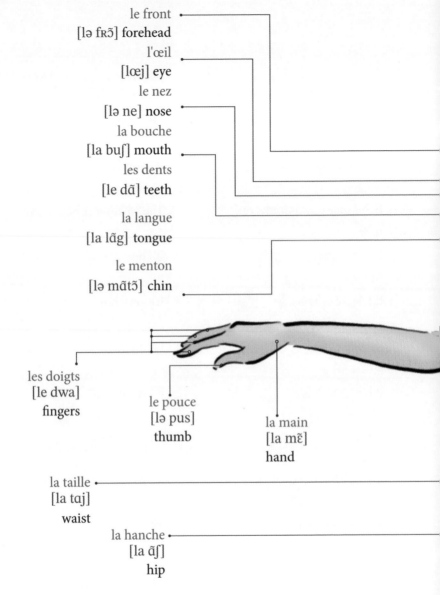

les doigts
[le dwa]
fingers

le pouce
[lə pus]
thumb

la main
[la mɛ̃]
hand

la taille
[la taj]
waist

la hanche
[la ɑ̃ʃ]
hip

Parts of the body

Les parties du corps [le paʀti dy kɔ:]

la tête
[la tɛt]
head

le visage
[lə vizaʒ]
face

l'oreille
[lɔʀɛj]
ear

la joue
[la ʒu]
cheek

le cou
[lə ku]
neck

la main
[la mɛ̃]
hand

l' épaule
[lepol]
shoulder

les cheveux
[le ʃəvø]
hair

le dos
[lə do]
back

le corps
[lə kɔʀ]
body

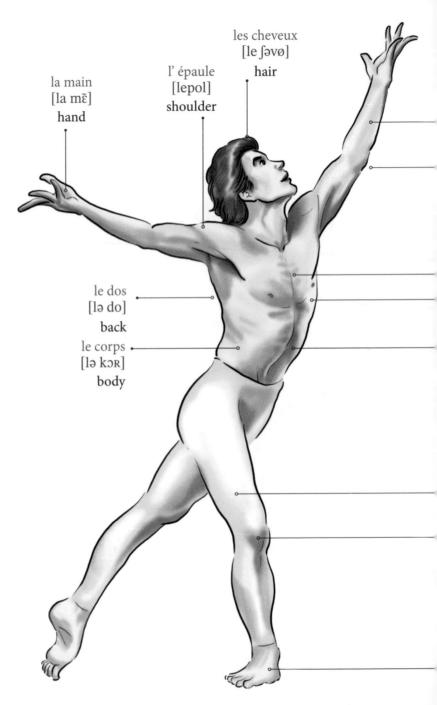

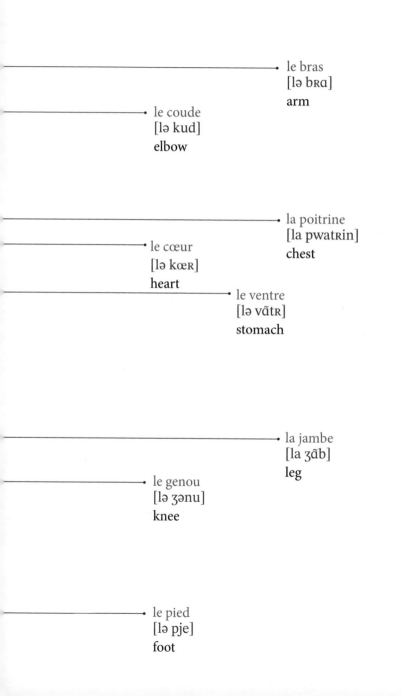

le bras
[lə bʀɑ]
arm

le coude
[lə kud]
elbow

la poitrine
[la pwatʀin]
chest

le cœur
[lə kœʀ]
heart

le ventre
[lə vɑ̃tʀ]
stomach

la jambe
[la ʒɑ̃b]
leg

le genou
[lə ʒənu]
knee

le pied
[lə pje]
foot

When you feel sick

Lorsque l'on est malade [lɔʀsk lɔ̃n_ɛ malad]

Je suis malade. [ʒə sɥi malad]	I don't feel well.
J'ai envie de vomir [ʒɛ ɑ̃vi də vɔmiʀ]	I need to vomit.
J'ai mal au cœur. [ʒɛ mal o kœʀ]	I feel nauseous.
J'ai mal ici. [ʒɛ mal isi]	It hurts here.
J'ai de la fièvre. [ʒɛ də la fjɛvʀ]	I have a fever.
J'ai mal à la tête. [ʒɛ mal a la tɛt]	I have a headache.
J'ai mal au ventre. [ʒɛ mal o vɑ̃tʀ]	I have a stomachache.

J'ai mal au cou.

[ʒɛ mal o ku]

I have a sore throat.

J'ai mal au dos.

[ʒɛ mal o do]

I have backache.

J'ai mal aux dents.

[ʒɛ mal o dɑ̃]

I have toothache.

Je suis constipé(e).

[ʒə sɥi kɔ̃stipe]

I am constipated.

J'ai la diarrhée.

[ʒɛ la djaʀe]

I have diarrhoea.

J'ai une allergie.

[ʒɛ yn alɛʀʒi]

I have an allergy.

J'ai des démangeaisons.
[ʒɛ de demɑ̃ʒɛzɔ̃]

I have an itch.

La pharmacie

[la faʀmasi] pharmacy

l'hôpital

[lɔpital] hospital

le médicament
[lə medikamɑ̃] medicine

le médecin
[lə medsɛ̃] doctor

le dentiste
[lə dɑ̃tist] dentist

l'ophtalmologiste

[lɔftalmɔlɔʒist] optometrist

le médecin généraliste

[lə medsɛ̃ ʒeneʀalist] general practitioner

le médecin d'urgences

[lə medsɛ̃ dyʀʒɑ̃s] emergency doctor

l'ambulance

[lɑ̃bylɑ̃s] ambulance

À tes souhaits !

[a te swɛ]

Bless you!

Urgency

Urgences [yʁʒɑ̃s]

Où sont les toilettes ?

[u sɔ̃ le twalɛt]

Where is the toilet?

J'ai besoin d'aller aux toilettes d'urgence.

[ʒɛ bəzwɛ̃ dale o twalɛt dyʁʒɑ̃s]

I need to go to the toilet urgently.

Est-ce qu'il y a des toilettes publiques ici ?

[ɛs‿kil‿ja de twalɛt pyblik isi]

Is there a public toilet near here?

Il faut que j'aille chez le médecin.

[il fo kə ʒaj ʃe lə medəsɛ̃]

I need to go to the doctor.

Appelez la police, s'il vous plaît !

[apɛle la pɔlis sil vu plɛ]

Call the police, please!

Attention !

[atɑ̃sjɔ̃]

Careful!

Au secours !

[o səkuʀ]

Help!

Au feu !

[o fø]

Fire!

Urgence !

[yʁʒɑ̃s]

Emergency!

What do these signs mean?

Que nous disent les panneaux ? [kə nu diz le pano]

ATTENTION

[atɑ̃sjɔ̃]

WARNING

SENS INTERDIT

[sɑ̃s_ɛ̃tɛʁdi]

NO ENTRY

ACCÈS INTERDIT

[aksɛ ɛ̃tɛʁdi]

RESTRICTED AREA

DANGER DE MORT

[dɑ̃ʒe dmɔʁ]

DANGER OF DEATH

DÉTOUR

[detuʁ]

DIVERSION

PARKING

[paʀkiŋ]

PARKING LOT

SENS UNIQUE

[sãs_ynik]

ONE WAY

STATIONNEMENT INTERDIT

[stasjɔnmã ɛ̃teʀdi]

NO PARKING

PRIÈRE DE NE PAS STATIONNER,
SORTIE DE VÉHICULES.

[pʀijɛʀ də npa stasjɔne
sɔʀti də veikyl]

PLEASE DO NOT PARK
VEHICLE EXIT

ACCÈS INTERDIT AUX
PERSONNES NON AUTORISÉES

[aksɛ ɛ̃teʀdi o pɛʀsɔn nɔ̃ ɔtɔʀize]

NO ACCESS TO
UNAUTHORIZED PERSONS

ATTENTION ÉCOLE

[atãsjɔ̃ ekɔl]

CAUTION
SCHOOL

ATTENTION! CHIEN MÉCHANT

[atɑ̃sjɔ̃ ʃjɛ̃ meʃɑ̃]

BEWARE OF THE DOG

RÉSERVÉ AUX RÉSIDENTS

[ʀezɛʀve o ʀezidɑ̃]

RESIDENT PARKING ONLY

PREMIERS SECOURS

[pʀəmje səkuʀ]

FIRST AID

MÉDECIN D'URGENCES

[medəsɛ̃ dyʀʒɑ̃s]

EMERGENCY DOCTOR

LA POSTE

[la pɔst]

POST OFFICE

PLAN D'ÉVACUATION

[plã devakyasjɔ̃]

EMERGENCY
EVACUATION PLAN

SORTIE DE SECOURS

[sɔʁti də səkuʁ]

FIRE EXIT

SORTIE D'URGENCE

[sɔʁti dyʁʒãs]

EMERGENCY EXIT

PERSONNEL AUTORISÉ
SEULEMENT

[pɛʁsɔnɛl ɔtɔʁize sœlmã]

AUTHORIZED PERSONNEL
ONLY

PASSAGE POUR PIÉTONS

[pɑsaʒ puʁ pjetɔnje]

PEDESTRIAN CROSSING

POUSSEZ

[puse]

PUSH

TIREZ

[tiʀe]

PULL

NE PAS DÉRANGER

[npa deʀɑ̃ʒe]

DO NOT DISTURB

DÉFENSE DE FUMER

[defɑ̃s də fyme]

NO SMOKING

TOILETTES DAMES

[twalɛt dam]

WOMEN'S TOILET

TOILETTES HOMMES

[twalɛt ɔm]

MEN'S TOILET

OUVERT

[uvɛʀ]

OPEN

FERMÉ

[fɛʀme]

CLOSED

LIBRE-SERVICE

[libʀ sɛʀvis]

SELF-SERVICE

RÉSERVÉ

[ʀezɛʀve]

RESERVED

NOURRITURE INTERDITE

[nuʀityʀ ɛ̃tɛʀdi]

NO FOOD OR DRINK ALLOWED

EMOTIONAL OUTBURSTS

In this chapter we will be dealing with something rather special: emotional outbursts. What, you may ask, does this have to do with a book aimed at introducing a foreign language?

I know that this is quite a sensitive issue and I'm pretty sure that you don't know any other language books that deal with the topic. As I say, I'm inviting you on a risky adventure. But I think it's absolutely essential for you and really useful. I think you need to know this because it can help you to avoid very embarrassing situations when you are in France.

First, let me explain what I mean by emotional outbursts. What exactly are they? They are words that simply tumble out of your mouth. You don't usually give them a second thought – they just pop out – and can't be popped back in again, once they're out.

When we are angry, disappointed, afraid, surprised or delighted, we use emotional outbursts to let off steam and regain our calm. We can think of them as turbulence tranquilizers for our emotions.

These outbursts can be more or less violent, depending on intonation and the particular intention or situation in which they are spoken. Gentle outbursts can be mumbled to ourselves to cool our spirits. Violent emotional outbursts are often insulting and deeply hurtful. This type is known in French as juron.

So, you can probably now appreciate how difficult and tricky this whole topic is. These words and phrases are used unconsciously all the time all over the world. The fact that I bring up this topic may be unpleasant for the French who are often reserved and polite by nature. However, my intentions are entirely good. I don't want to insult or ridicule their language, but simply to help you avoid making a fool of yourself.

If you hear these French words and try to copy them, it's more than likely that you'll get the exact intonation wrong, or it won't come out at quite the right moment, or be appropriate for the person or situation you're in.

So, my first tip is: don't block your ears when you hear them, but don't just copy them either. As a foreigner, you need to get to know them but use them carefully, and only if you're absolutely certain about how and when.

But even if you never use these outbursts yourself, it is certainly helpful to know them. It might avoid a few embarrassing situations or even a slap around the face. This is one of the main reasons for dealing with these phrases.

I hope I've been able to make clear why this topic is an important one in language learning.

Now let's get started:

The first word we need to get to know is: "Merde!"

This word describes the end product of your digestive system, and we use the corresponding word in English, but it would be impolite to use the direct translation here. You know the word I mean. (After all, this is a respectable publication and not a cheap newspaper.) Everyone knows this word, and there are equivalents all over the world. So, I need say no more!

The next word the French use to let off steam is "Putain!"

The literal translation refers to a lady whose profession involves a lot of lying down, but that's not usually what the French mean when they use this outburst. He (or she) probably doesn't even think about ladies when using the word. It is usually used to express anger or frustration with the current situation or with a particular person.

Now let's turn to the French word "Patate!"

This word can be directly translated as "potato". It is in fact commonly used in this context and is as such not in any way rude. However, if the word is used with a clear undertone of anger, it suggests the speaker thinks the person he is speaking to is crazy, or just plain stupid. In this context it is clearly an insult.

"Ta guele!" is the next phrase, which literally means "your snout". Since we refer to the thing we eat and speak with normally as a "mouth" and only use "snout" for animals, this phrase is also an emotional outburst. What the speaker really means is: "I'd be much happier if you don't say another word."

The alternative expression would be "La ferme !" the equivalent meaning in English is "shut up!"

Dealing with the next words is an even more sensitive issue. Any decent Frenchman reading them might be horrified and see it as an insult to their beautiful language. As I have already said, this is not my intention in writing this book. In order to respect their feelings, I have decided to use a kind of code. I will not write the word itself but use the phonetic alphabet. This also has the useful side effect that you will learn how to spell the words.

The first of these words is Suzanne, Anatole, Louis, Oscar, Pierre, Eugène. This word is a curse word that refers to women who are easy to invite to bed. Whether the speaker really knows the nightly habits of the lady in question is not important here. Sometimes the word is use in the literal sense and at other times figuratively. Whichever way it's used, it's an insult and not a pleasant way to express your feelings for a lady.

There is a corresponding word that applies to men: Suzanne, Anatole, Louis, Oscar, Pierre, Anatole, Raoul, Désiré.

The man who receives this insult is certainly not seen in a good light. It suggests he is unfaithful to his wife. He is having an affair and is definitely not to be trusted. If the word is used in a very strong way, it suggests a comparison between him and the muscle at the end of his digestive system.

"Sa...... !"

The following phrase is made up of two words. It's a curse word that describes the son of a lady, whose profession involves a lot of lying down. Actually, the speaker knows neither the son nor his mother. It is simply a way of expressing extreme distaste and disrespect to the person you are addressing.

The words in code are:

François, Irma, Louis, Suzanne,
Désiré, Eugène,
Pierre, Ursule, Thérèse, Eugène

Finally, we need to turn to the really bad French curse words. If you really want to hurt someone badly, we often use words or phrases from a sexual context. This is actually rather surprising. After all, the sexes are also a context in which we experience love and attraction. But that's the way it is. I'm not here to comment on whether that's good or bad. My role is to stay neutral and tell you the facts.

Words in this category are used very often in France. They cannot be translated word for word because the definition doesn't have a lot to do with what the speaker means. And if we're honest, we will soon realise that we have similar words in our own language.

The first word in this extreme category is Célestin, Oscar, Nicolas.

This is a vulgar word for the female genitalia. Whatever the reason may be for using this otherwise highly desirable part of a woman's body as a swear word, the outburst itself does not refer to female anatomy at all. Depending on the context, it means:

1) in its weaker form, we use it to refer to someone who we consider to be unintellegent or who acts stupidly.

2) in its stronger form, we are comparing the person in question to the exit of our digestive system.

The second word in this extreme category is Célestin, Oscar, Nicolas, Nicolas, Eugène.

Finally, dear readers, let me assure you that I have tried to do all I can to deal with such a sensitive and controversial issue without embarrassing you. I strongly believe that it is important to give you as much confidence as possible when starting to learn the French language.

Knowing something about how people express their feelings and emotions is part of that process. I could continue this theme for some time, but it's enough for you to have a clear idea of the topic, so that you can avoid any embarrassing situations.

Never forget that emotional outbursts can vary in meaning as well as in intensity. They are used by all levels of society, and you'll find them used both by fine old society ladies and socially-deprived youngsters.

If you hear one of these phrases, see if you can hear whether the speaker is angry, dissatisfied, furious, or perhaps cracking a joke or making fun of someone. As far as possible, avoid using these outbursts yourself. Remember that these words have the power to insult and hurt others and can also be dangerous for you. By using them you are likely to put yourself in a very embarrassing situation, and quite possibly lose face in the process.

Bravo !
[bʀavo]
Bravo!

Super !
[sypɛʀ]
Super!

Génial !
[ʒenjal]
Great!

Parfait !
[paʀfɛ]
Perfect!

Compliments

Les compliments [le kɔ̃plimɑ̃]

C'est magnifique !

[sɛ maɲifik]

That's magnificent!

C'est merveilleux !

[sɛ mɛʀvɛjø]

That's wonderful!

Romance

Un peu de romantisme [ɛ̃ pø də ʀɔmɑ̃tism]

Tu es tellement belle/beau.
[ty ɛ tɛlmɑ̃ bɛl bo]
You are so beautiful.

Tu as des beaux yeux.
[ty a de boz‿jø]
You have beautiful eyes.

Tu es unique.
[ty ɛ ynik]
You are unique.

Je t'aime bien.
[ʒə tɛm bjɛ̃]
I like you.

Je t'aime beaucoup.
[ʒə tɛm boku]
I love you very much.

Tu es incroyablement belle.

[ty ɛ ɛ̃kʀwajabləmɑ̃ bɛl]

You are incredibly beautiful.

Tu es extraordinaire.

[ty ɛ ɛkstraɔʀdinɛʀ]

You are amazing.

Je t'aime.

[ʒə teɪm]

I love you.

Veux-tu m'épouser ?

[vø-ty mepuze]

Will you marry me?

Tu es ravissante.

[ty ɛ ʀavisɑ̃t]

You are gorgeous.

Land and people

Le pays et les gens [lə pei e le ʒɑ̃]

If you want to learn about the shape and form of France, the simplest thing to do is to look at a map. If you want to know more about the people, how they think, how they lead their lives, then the best method is to look at their proverbs. They reveal how the French tick.

Often proverbs have developed over centuries as the result of local people's experiences and of the way they think and live their lives. These sayings are passed on from one generation to the next, together with the emotions and moods they convey. Here are a few memorable French proverbs:

Chaque chose en son temps.
[ʃak ʃoz‿ɑ̃ sɔ̃ tɑ̃]
Everything in its time.

Chacun est l'artisan de sa fortune.
[ʃakœ̃ ɛ laʀtizɑ̃ də sa fɔʀtyn]
Everyone is the architect of their own fortune.

Mauvaise herbe pousse toujours.
[mɔvɛ ɛʀb pus tuʒuʀ]
Weed always grows.

Après la pluie vient le beau temps.
[apʀɛ la plɥi vjɛ̃ lə bo tɑ̃]
After the rain comes the rainbow.

Tout est bien qui finit bien.
[tu ɛ bjɛ̃ ki finit bjɛ̃]
All's well that ends well.

Now you will be able to savour the French language like a delicatessen. Any worries you may have had about learning this language will turn to joyful confidence.

French
at your Fingertips

by
Tien Tammada

Original title: ฝรั่งเศสทันใจพูดได้ด้วยปลายนิ้ว เซียร ธรรมดา
© Leelaaphasa Co.,Ltd.
63/120 Moo 8, Tambon Saothonghin, Bangyai District,
Nonthaburi 11140 Thailand
E-Mail: leelaaphasa2008@gmail.com
All rights reserved.

1. Edition 2023 (1,01 - 2023)
© PONS Langenscheidt GmbH, Stöckachstraße 11, 70190 Stuttgart, 2023

Translation: Ta Tammadien, David Thron
Proofreaders: Dr. Nathalie Karanfilovic, Klangjai Patanant
Cover Design: Sira Illner, Leonie Eul
Illustrationen Inside: K. Kiattisak, Netitorn Terdbankird,
Purmpoon Khamnuanta
Bildnachweis Cover: arc de triomphe, perfume bottle: Shutterstock, Natalya
Levish; french flag: K. Klattisak; bicycle: Getty Images, Grafner
Typesetting/Layout: Wachana Leuwattananon, Vipoo Lerttasanawanish
Printing: Multiprint GmbH, Konstinbrod

ISBN 978-3-12-514554-2